Introduction

West Midlands Passanger Transport Executive (WMPTE) first came into existence in 1969. It was formed by the joining together of various West Midlands Corporation companies, these being Birmingham City Transport, West Bromwich, Walsall and Wolverhampton. Later on, Coventry Transport was also included.

Known as 'Wumpty' by locals, WMPTE chose to adopt the livery used by the largest of its inherited fleet – Birmingham City Transport – and so blue and cream was the livery to be worn by all the fleets from across the different areas.

The different former fleets were split into divisions, with the Birmingham area being the South Division, while Walsall, West Bromwich and Wolverhampton became known as the North Division and Coventry became the East Division.

In 1973, part of the old Midland Red empire came under the WMPTE wing, and so transferred in a whole host of Midland Red vehicles.

WMPTE decided to standardise its diverse fleet by ordering large numbers of Daimler- and later Leyland-built Fleetlines. They were bodied by Park Royal as well as by local bus builder Metro Cammell Weymann (MCW). Large numbers of Leyland-built Nationals were also ordered to standardise the single-deck fleet. These large intakes of buses helped to make a start in eliminating the older fleet.

In 1978 WMPTE ordered five MCW-bodied Metrobuses and five Park Royal-bodied Leyland Titans. The MCW product would be chosen to be the new flag-bearer for the West Midlands, with over 1,000 being ordered.

In October 1986 the government decided to deregulate the bus networks across the country, and so the assets of WMPTE transferred to a new company – West Midlands Travel. A start was soon made in rebranding the buses and some new networks were set up as soon as deregulation had occurred. The Mini Buzz network sprang up, and also the superb Timesaver network of coach-seated, limited stop routes using brand-new MCW Metrobuses. A large fleet of Leyland Lynxes would soon be acquired as well to start eliminating the Leyland National fleet. West Midlands Travel also adopted a new silver livery, which would replace the traditional blue and cream.

1986 would also see the closure of many of the smaller garages, with more effort placed on creating larger garages.

West Midlands Travel was still in public ownership and was sold in 1991 to the management and employees, known as the ESOP (Employee Share Ownership Plan). To celebrate, each garage had a bus painted in a special ESOP green livery.

The next name change came in the early 1990s, when the fleet started to gain WM Buses fleetnames that also incorporated the home garage of the vehicle. This would only last a few years, as West Midlands Travel would merge with National Express and become Travel West Midlands.

With the arrival of low-floor buses, a serious inroad was started in eliminating the older fleet. All the Fleetlines had been withdrawn by 1997 and all the Leyland Lynxes and MCW Metrobuses have also been retired, leaving just a low-floor fleet. Travel West Midlands was further rebranded, becoming National Express West Midlands.

This book intends to take the reader on a journey from the 1970s WMPTE days through to the Travel West Midlands era of the early 2000s. It also intends to show how the different types of vehicles changed during those years, but doesn't include any low-floor buses. I hope the reader enjoys browsing through this book as much as I have enjoyed compiling it.

I would like to say a special thank you to Chris Clarke and also Keith Billingsley for some valuable assistance. I would like to dedicate this book to my late father, Anthony Cole, who worked for over thirty years at Washwood Heath, and Lea Hall garages, whose early photographs I have used in this book.

No. 3332, 332 GON
No. 3332 is seen climbing the Alum Rock Road while on route 55 to Shard End. This MCW-bodied Daimler Fleetline was allocated to Washwood Heath garage at the time, and this view shows typically what WMPTE came to inherit. No. 3332 carries Birmingham City Transport blue and cream livery, which WMPTE didn't alter too drastically.

West Midlands PTE

No. 116, XDH 516G

No. 116, a Northern Counties-bodied Daimler Fleetline, is seen at Wythall carrying WMPTE blue and cream livery. This was delivered new to Walsall Corporation and has been preserved by the Birmingham and Midland Motor Omnibus Trust (BaMMOT), Wythall.

No. 367Y, CRW 367C

No. 367Y is seen parked outside Washwood Heath garage ready for a turn on the 26. This was a Willowbrook-bodied Daimler Fleetline that was new to Coventry Corporation, and was on loan to the South Division along with several other members of the Coventry fleet. They were only on loan for a short time between 1978 and 1979. No. 367Y would later become No. 1367.

No. 516, HOC 516W

No. 516, a Ford A-Series Dormobile, is seen parked outside the back of Perry Barr garage. This was one of twenty of these unusual vehicles operated by WMPTE and were equipped with wheelchair lifts for transporting the disabled. None of these buses survived in service past deregulation in 1986.

No. 1010, AOL 10T

No. 1010 is seen parked outside the front of Perry Barr garage carrying standard WMPTE blue and cream livery. This Leyland National was part of a small batch of ten that were delivered in plain cream livery, and No. 1010 was delivered carrying the number 7010.

No. 1051, DOC 51V

No. 1051 is seen carrying all-over advert livery for Virgin Megastore. This Leyland National Mk 2 was from a batch of just five that were shorter than the normal Nationals and were used mainly on the 101 Centrebus route around Birmingham City Centre. Most carried all-over advert liveries.

No. 1052, DOC 52V

No. 1052 carries all-over advert livery for Smithfield Audi Volkswagen while parked outside Perry Barr garage. This Mk 2 Leyland National was delivered as No. 7052 but was renumbered, along with the rest of the single-deck fleet, into the 1xxx number series.

No. 1053, B53 AOC

No. 1053 is seen at Pool Meadow bus station, Coventry. This was one of a pair of Duple-bodied Dennis Lancet buses ordered by WMPTE for Easy Rider services in Coventry. Both were fitted with wheelchair ramps and both suited the WMPTE livery superbly. No. 1053 had been delivered as No. 7053.

No. 1059, C59 HOM

No. 1059 is seen taking part in the Sandwell bus rally. This Alexander-bodied Volvo Citybus was one of six delivered to WMPTE for evaluation purposes and is seen in as-delivered white and blue livery.

No. 1066, C66 HOM

No. 1066 rests inside Cleveland Road garage, Wolverhampton. This Leyland Lynx was part of a small batch of six pre-production Lynxes delivered alongside six Volvo Citybuses as trial vehicles. The Lynx would prove to be the successful of the two, with an order for 250 Lynxes to follow.

No. 1097, YVC 97K

No. 1097 can be seen to the right in this photograph taken at the Adderley Road dumping ground opposite Liverpool Street garage. Buses would end up here prior to being sold to scrap dealers. Also in the shot are standard Fleetlines, Bristol VRTs, ex-London DMSs, and other ex-Coventry Fleetlines. Today this piece of land has been concreted over and is used as part of Birmingham Central garage.

No. 1105, YVC 105K

No. 1105 heads a line-up of other East Lancs-bodied Daimler Fleetlines inside Sandy Lane garage, Coventry. This bus unusually carries a Harnall Lane 'H' above the windscreen, instead of a Sandy Lane 'S'.

No. 1109, YVC 109K

No. 1109, an East Lancs-bodied Daimler Fleetline, is seen parked inside Sandy Lane garage, Coventry, alongside No. 2109, a MCW-bodied Metrobus. Sandy Lane garage had all the odd-numbered buses in Coventry, whereas Harnall Lane had the even-numbered allocation.

No. 1124, PDU 124M

No. 1124 is seen withdrawn out the back of Harnall Lane garage, Coventry. It is seen alongside fellow East Lancs-bodied Daimler Fleetline No. 1102.

No. 1131, GWK 131L

No. 1131 is seen parked alongside Sandy Lane garage, Coventry. This garage used to house a ring of buses around the outside on Sundays, and also housed a works, which carried out mid-life overhauls of some Fleetlines. Of note with No. 1131 are the big Daimler badge on the front and the white steering wheel.

No. 1133, PDU 133M

No. 1133 is seen parked up at Pool Meadow bus station, Coventry. This is another East Lancs-bodied Daimler Fleetline that carried a Harnall Lane 'H' above the windscreen, whereas all the odd-numbered buses in Coventry were based at Sandy Lane.

No. 1483, TOE 483N

No. 1483 is seen parked outside a frosty Walsall garage. This had recently been renumbered from 4483, and of note are the withdrawn MCW-bodied Bristol VRTs alongside. The building in the background is used today by National Express West Midlands as their paint shop.

West Midlands PTE and Its Successors

No. 1506, TOE 506N

No. 1506 is seen parked outside the front of the impressive-looking West Bromwich garage. This garage, located in Oak Lane, was opened to buses in 1929 by West Bromwich Corporation Transport.

No. 1790, KOM 790P

No. 1790, a dual-door Leyland National, is seen parked in the yard at Dudley alongside MCW-bodied Leyland Fleetline No. 6788. No. 1790 was one of only twelve dual-door MK 1 Nationals operated by WMPTE.

No. 1824, OOX 824R

No. 1824 is seen parked outside the front of Perry Barr garage carrying the attractive dual-purpose single-deck livery. WMPTE ordered thirty dual-purpose Leyland Nationals for limited stop services and for private hires.

No. 2002, BOK 2V

No. 2002 is seen on the fuel pumps at Selly Oak garage having run in. This was the second production MCW-bodied Metrobus, and even by this early stage had lost both of its front fog lamps. The original production Metrobus, No. 2001, has been preserved. Selly Oak garage received the first fifteen Metrobuses to help eliminate some older Fleetlines.

No. 2007, BOK 7V
No. 2007 is seen standing over one of the pits inside Selly Oak garage alongside fellow Metrobus No. 2148. Of note are the different front grilles used by both Metrobuses, and also the differently shaped fog lamps used by both.

No. 2012, BOK 12V
No. 2012 heads a row of other MCW-bodied Metrobuses inside Selly Oak garage. No. 2004 can be seen to the left, which was withdrawn in 1990 following collision damage. When Selly Oak closed, the first fifteen Metrobuses transferred to Walsall garage to cover for the withdrawal of the MCW-bodied Bristol VRTs.

No. 2020, BOK 20V

No. 2020 is seen in the yard at Acocks Green garage having just been released from works overhaul. The work involved having a special advert painted onto the bus for Sabaco LTD. No. 2020 was allocated to Sandy Lane garage, Coventry, at the time.

No. 2025, BOK 25V

No. 2025 is seen at a very gloomy Pool Meadow bus station, Coventry. The bus is in as-delivered condition, with a black painted skirt and front grille. After Selly Oak received the first fifteen MCW Metrobuses, the two Coventry garages then shared the next sixteen.

No. 2079, BOK 79V

No. 2079 is seen inside Quinton garage carrying, like so many other WMPTE buses at the time, an advert warning about the threat of deregulation. No. 2079 formed part of the second batch of MCW Metrobuses, which totalled 150 buses.

No. 2163, GOG 163W

No. 2163 is seen parked in the layover bay at Pool Meadow bus station, Coventry. No. 2163 carries an all-over advert for Robinson, Osborne & Moules, chartered surveyors. The two Coventry garages shared a small batch of thirteen Metrobuses in the No. 2156 to No. 2168 number range, and all of these Metrobuses seemed to carry all-over adverts at some time of another.

No. 2181, GOG 181W

No. 2181 is seen in High Street, Birmingham, carrying an all-over advert for British Telecom. This MCW-bodied Metrobus was allocated to Acocks Green at the time and was right at home on the 37.

No. 2185, GOG 185W

No. 2185 is seen parked waiting to leave Washwood Heath garage. This Metrobus carries a half-advert livery for the Co-op, and another bus to carry this livery was No. 2442. There were also similar Tesco-painted Metrobuses in Coventry.

No. 2198, GOG 198W

No. 2198 is seen parked at Pool Meadow bus station, Coventry. Being an even-numbered Metrobus, this would have been allocated to Harnall Lane garage at the time. No. 2198 is seen in as-delivered condition with the black skirt and front grille, which were later painted blue to match the rest of the bus.

No. 2215, GOG 215W

No. 2215 is seen parked in the yard of Coventry Road garage carrying an all-over advert for the 1984 West Midlands Peace Year. There were certainly plenty of all-over-advert-liveried Metrobuses around during this period.

No. 2276, KJW 276W

No. 2276 is seen on the old fuel pumps inside Washwood Heath garage carrying an all-over advert for Johnstone's Paints. No. 2276 has the 11 Outer Circle on the blinds, but Washwood Heath didn't have any running boards for the Outer Circle, so presumably this was a change bus.

No. 2284, KJW 284W

No. 2284 rests outside the front of Washwood Heath garage carrying all-over advert livery for Jockey Shorts. This was on loan at the time from Perry Barr, along with No. 2283, which carried adverts for Y-Fronts.

No. 2316, KJW 316W
No. 2316 is seen parked outside Cotteridge garage advertising Birmingham City Markets. Of note are the old tram tracks still in situ at this garage.

No. 2444, NOA 444X
No. 2444 stands outside Oldbury garage. This MCW Metrobus was part of the first order of the Mk 2 Metrobuses, and after the initial few were allocated to West Bromwich, Oldbury then received the next few.

No. 2458, NOA 458X

No. 2458 is seen parked inside Harnall Lane garage, Coventry. The two Coventry garages shared a strange way of allocating their vehicles, with Harnall Lane having the even-numbered buses, and Sandy Lane all the odd-numbered buses. No. 2458 carries all-over advert livery for WM Travelcard.

No. 2498, POG 498Y

No. 2498 is seen when brand new outside Washwood Heath garage. No. 2498 had just left the MCW factory in Common Lane and would be delivered to Wolverhampton. Of note is that it is travelling on trade plates and already has the ticket machine and cash vault fitted.

No. 2536, POG 536Y

No. 2536 is seen parked in the yard of Cotteridge garage. This garage, like a few others, kept some tram tracks right up until the garage closed.

No. 2700, A700 UOE

No. 2700 is seen parked inside Walsall garage surrounded by other MCW Metrobuses and a Volvo Ailsa. Of note is the lack of adverts on any of the buses.

No. 2820, JOJ 820

No. 2820 is seen at Washwood Heath carrying Travelcard livery. After its service career had finished, this Crossley-bodied Daimler CVG6 took up use as a mobile Travelcard sales office. Of note is brand new Leyland Titan No. 7001 alongside.

No. 2882, B882 DOM

No. 2882 is seen parked next to the fuel pumps at Selly Oak garage after running in from a turn on the night bus. No. 2882 was part of the last batch of MCW-bodied Metrobuses delivered to WMPTE, the last being No. 2910, delivered to Washwood Heath.

No. 3245, 245 DOC

No. 3245 is seen parked at Walsall garage when its service career had finished and it was in use as a driver trainer. This was one of the earliest MCW-bodied Daimler Fleetlines used by WMPTE and it's such a shame that it didn't survive into preservation as it outlasted its sisters by quite a few years.

No. 3258, 258 GON

No. 3258 is seen parked alongside the old part of Washwood Heath garage. No. 3258 is a Park Royal-bodied Daimler Fleetline and this view shows the more rounded styling used in the early Fleetlines. Where No. 3258 stands was where the newer part of Washwood Heath was to be built.

No. 3867, NOV 867G

No. 3867 is seen in Wellhead Lane, Perry Barr garage, during the garage's open day in 1985. No. 3867 was converted to an open-top bus after hitting a railway bridge and was later sold. WMPTE also had another open-top Fleetline in the form of No. 4069.

No. 3975, SOE 975H

No. 3975 is seen parked in the yard at Washwood Heath. This was one of the 124 Park Royal-bodied 'Jumbo' Fleetlines that all had short lives in the West Midlands. They were some of the last buses delivered with just a single-line destination screen, their main Achilles heel being the bodywork around the centre exit. None were allocated to Washwood Heath, and this one was on loan.

No. 4065, YOX 65K

No. 4065 stands outside the crowded front of Washwood Heath garage. This part of the garage had only recently opened, and No. 4065 was on loan from Harborne garage at the time. Of note is that No. 4065 carries the old black-style number plate, and still retains a khaki-coloured roof.

No. 4106, YOX 106K

No. 4106 is seen parked inside Stourbridge garage, Brierley Hill. This view shows No. 4106 in typical WMPTE condition – clean and respectable with no dents or scratches to be seen. Stourbridge garage would close in 1985.

No. 4145, YOX 145K

No. 4145 is seen standing in the yard at Coventry Road garage, alongside No. 4146. Both of these MCW-bodied Daimler Fleetlines were sold for scrap. Coventry Road garage was closed upon deregulation in 1986 but still stands today, although in private use.

No. 4170, YOX 170K

No. 4170 is seen parked in the yard at Miller Street garage. No. 4170 still carries the old black-style number plate, whereas No. 4213 alongside has received a new white version. Miller Street is still in use today, although it is used for storing withdrawn buses prior to sending them to the scrapyards, or for resale.

No. 4254, EOF 254L

No. 4254 is seen parked inside the cramped garage at Cotteridge. This was a former tram depot that opened in 1904 and was unable to expand due to the railway lines behind and shops alongside, and it therefore closed in 1986.

No. 4262, EOF 262L

No. 4262 is seen outside the front of Washwood Heath garage alongside No. 6650 during the time that the garage was being rebuilt. This view shows the two different styles of lettering applied to the fronts at this time. Both of these Fleetlines were bodied by Park Royal.

No. 4266, EOF 266L

No. 4266 is seen outside the front of Lea Hall garage, Kitts Green. This was during the time that Washwood Heath was being rebuilt, and due to space constraints some buses had to be parked at Lea Hall to create space. Buses were never normally parked in this area of the garage.

No. 4300, EOF 300L

No. 4300 is seen parked inside Harborne garage. This was another small garage that would close in 1986, along with plenty of others around this time. No. 4300 was a Park Royal-bodied Daimler Fleetline and would end up working for Black Prince of Morley.

No. 4338, NOB 338M

No. 4338 is seen withdrawn outside Cotteridge garage. This Park Royal-bodied Daimler Fleetline had been withdrawn due to collision damage it received to its rear end and a start has already been made in stripping it for spare parts.

No. 4342, NOB 342M

No. 4342 spends a Sunday afternoon parked inside the garage at Cotteridge. It is about to receive a new advert on the side, and it was the last, numerically, of a large batch of Park Royal-bodied Daimler Fleetlines.

No. 4347, EOF 347L

No. 4347 rests outside Walsall garage. This MCW-bodied Bristol VRT was from a batch of 100 ordered by WMPTE. These buses were to prove to be not very successful, with the majority having only short lives in the West Midlands and most being sold to National Welsh. The other batch of 100 didn't fare much better, all being withdrawn by 1986.

No. 4453, ROK 453M

No. 4453 is seen parked in the familiar setting of Pool Meadow bus station, Coventry. This East Lancs-bodied Daimler Fleetline is from a small batch of twenty such vehicles. Of note is the fact the other two Fleetlines have lost their WMPTE logos, while No. 4453 has kept them, as it was going to be withdrawn by deregulation day in October 1986.

No. 4527, TOE 527N
No. 4527 is seen outside Perry Barr garage, having been withdrawn from service. This was the first of three prototype Alexander-bodied Volvo Ailsa AB57s that were ordered by WMPTE, and their success lead to an order of fifty Volvo Ailsa B55-10s. No. 4527 was happily preserved and is today in the care of the 4738 Group.

No. 4529, TOE 529N
No. 4529 stands withdrawn outside Walsall Works. This was from a batch of three prototype Volvo Ailsa AB57s ordered by WMPTE. This batch had slightly different body features compared to the production batch, having a 'rounder' appearance and a different lower front body styling, with the indicators mounted above the windscreens.

No. 4610, JOV 610P

No. 4610 stands next to the bus wash in the yard at Dudley garage. This garage was closed and demolished in 1993 to make way for the Dudley by-pass. No. 4610 carries an advert regarding the deregulation of bus services, which happened in 1986.

No. 4665, GOG 665N

No. 4665 is seen parked outside Walsall garage underneath an impressive Walsall Corporation Motors façade. No. 4665 was from a batch of 100 MCW-bodied Bristol VRTs, and they spent most, if not all of their working lives based at Walsall. All of the fleet was withdrawn by deregulation in October 1986.

No. 4670, GOG 670N

No. 4670 is seen parked outside the back of Walsall garage. By this time large-scale withdrawals of the MCW-bodied Bristol VRT fleet was underway, with many examples being dispatched to the scrapyards of Barnsley, although a few did find new owners.

No. 4719, JOV 719P

No. 4719 stands outside the back of Walsall garage. This MCW-bodied Bristol VRT would go on to work for Wilts & Dorset, based in Poole, becoming No. 3471 in their fleet.

No. 4721, JOV 721P

No. 4721 is seen parked outside the front of Walsall garage. This was another of the fourteen members of this 100-strong batch of MCW-bodied Bristol VRTs that found their way to Wilts & Dorset, becoming No. 3472 in their fleet.

No. 4740, JOV 740P

No. 4740 is seen parked in the yard at a frosty Walsall garage. Fifty of these Alexander-bodied Volvo Ailsa B55-10s were ordered by WMPTE, being based initially at Oldbury and Sutton Coldfield garages. They were unusual in the WMPTE fleet in having front engines, rather than at the rear.

No. 4742, JOV 742P

No. 4742 is seen standing outside Oldbury garage, along with several classmates. This was another small depot, which closed before deregulation. Most of the fifty Volvo Ailsas later transferred to Walsall, and then Perry Barr garages, before finally being sold off to London Buses.

No. 4745, JOV 745P

No. 4745 leads an impressive line-up of Alexander-bodied Volvo Ailsa B55-10s at Walsall garage. These buses were transferred into Walsall to help eliminate the Bristol VRT buses, which were not to survive deregulation in 1986. The Ailsas later transferred en masse to Perry Barr garage.

No. 4762, JOV 762P

No. 4762 is seen parked outside the now demolished Oldbury garage. This garage transferred to WMPTE use from Midland Red, but was closed prior to deregulation in 1986.

No. 4785, JOV 785P

No. 4785 is seen parked outside Walsall Works, having just been released from overhaul. This view shows the graceful lines of these distinctive buses and it's a shame that many more were never ordered.

No. 4791, KOM 791P

No. 4791 is seen parked inside Lea Hall garage, Kitts Green. This Leyland National is one of the twelve dual-door examples that were ordered for use around the National Exhibition Centre, and when new they carried a special red, white and blue livery. No. 4791 would go on to be renumbered 1791.

No. 4799, KOM 799P

No. 4799 is seen standing outside the back of Acocks Green garage, along with fellow withdrawn National No. 4798. Both of these dual-door Leyland Nationals had been withdrawn for a while, and neither would be renumbered.

No. 5103, HHA 103L

No. 5103 is seen parked in the yard at Lea Hall garage, Kitts Green. This Leyland National was one of thirty-three that were transferred to WMPTE from Midland Red in 1973 out of a batch of fifty-eight. These Nationals were instantly recognisable by being in the 51xx number range.

No. 5105, HHA 105L

No. 5105 is seen up on the jacks inside Lea Hall garage, Kitts Green. This was another ex-Midland Red Leyland National and none of the batch would survive past deregulation in 1986.

No. 5152, HHA 152L
No. 5152 is seen parked inside Stourbridge garage alongside sister Leyland National No. 4481. Despite only being two years older, all of the former Midland Red Nationals were withdrawn by the end of 1986, while the WMPTE examples had much longer lives.

No. 5516, JGU 279K
No. 5516 is seen parked on the forecourt of Selly Oak garage. WMPTE purchased eighty redundant MCW-bodied Daimler Fleetlines from London Transport, refurbishing them and putting them back into service. These former 'DMS' buses gave sterling service while based in the Midlands, and No. 5516 was formerly DMS1279.

No. 5534, MLH 310L

No. 5534 is seen standing outside Washwood Heath garage. This was formerly London Transport DMS1310, and like all the other ex-London Fleetlines it was converted from dual-door to single-door before being put into service.

No. 5555, MLH 336L

No. 5555 is seen outside Washwood Heath garage. Washwood Heath never had an allocation of former London DMS Fleetlines; the majority were based at Harborne, Quinton, Selly Oak and Yardley Wood, where No. 5555 was visiting from. No. 5555 was formerly DMS1336 in the London Transport fleet.

No. 5557, MLH 338L

No. 5557 is seen at rest inside its home garage of Yardley Wood, alongside sister No. 5548. Both of these MCW-bodied Daimler Fleetlines came to the West Midlands from London Transport, with No. 5548 being renumbered from DMS1327 while No. 5557 was ex-DMS1338.

No. 6357, KON 357P

No. 6357 spends a lazy Sunday afternoon parked in the yard at Harts Hill garage, Brierley Hill. Harts Hill was a small garage in terms of size and like so many others it too has been closed. No. 6357 was an MCW-bodied Leyland Fleetline.

No. 6500, NOC 500R

No. 6500 is seen parked inside Park Lane garage, Wolverhampton. By this time, this MCW-bodied Leyland Fleetline had gained the full West Midlands logo on the front instead of just the 'WM'. Park Lane garage would close in 1986 but it would later reopen and it is today the main garage for the Wolverhampton fleet.

No. 6511, SDA 511S

No. 6511 is seen parked in the yard at Lea Hall garage, Kitts Green. No. 6511 had not long been through works for overhaul, with its paintwork still gleaming.

No. 6544, SDA 544S

No. 6544 is seen in the yard at Dudley garage alongside No. 6376. This view shows the new logo applied to the front of No. 6544, compared to the more traditional logo on the front of No. 6376. Both of these Leyland Fleetlines carry MCW bodywork.

No. 6758, SDA 758S

No. 6758 stands proudly in the yard at Harnall Lane garage, Coventry. This East Lancs-bodied Leyland Fleetline has not long been through the workshops, as the paintwork still gives off a shine. Of note is the new logo on the front and the Harnall Lane 'H' above the driver's windscreen.

No. 6816, OOX 816R

No. 6816 is seen standing on the pits at Washwood Heath garage. This dual-purpose Leyland National was just passing through, as Washwood Heath never had an allocation of Nationals, and the missing lower blind indicates that No. 6816 was being transferred around the system. No. 6816 later became No. 1816 when it was renumbered.

No. 6831, SDA 831S

No. 6831 is seen standing inside Washwood Heath having just received a repaint. This was the very first MCW Metrobus delivered to WMPTE and it was based at Washwood Heath, not too far from its birthplace. This Metrobus was the only one in the fleet to have a side seat above the nearside front wheel, similar to the Fleetlines, and it also boasted red seats and blue Formica. It would eventually be transferred to Dudley along with the other four preproduction Metros in this batch.

No. 6834, SDA 834S

No. 6834 is seen parked at Dudley bus station. This view shows the red seats and blue Formica off a treat, which only the first four of this batch and the two Rolls-Royce prototypes carried. Also of note is the cream stripe that doesn't go fully around the back of the bus, a feature that didn't last too long.

No. 6955, WDA 955T

No. 6955 rests inside Washwood Heath garage having just been through works overhaul, including having the lighter shade of blue applied. This was right at the very end of WMPTE operation, as this blue was only applied to West Midlands Travel vehicles, although it still carries WMPTE legal lettering.

No. 6956, WDA 956T

No. 6956 is seen parked inside Washwood Heath garage, complete with new-style fleetnames on the front. This MCW-bodied Leyland Fleetline would go on to gain notoriety by being chosen to be rebuilt as a single-deck bus. It still survives today in preservation.

No. 6999, WDA 999T

No. 6999 is seen parked in the yard at Dudley garage surrounded by other Fleetlines. No. 6999 was an MCW-bodied Leyland example and of note is the running number on the offside still in its original position, not yet having been moved to above the driver's window.

No. 7001, WDA 1T

No. 7001 is seen parked outside Washwood Heath when brand new. WMPTE ordered five Park Royal-bodied Leyland Titans at the same time that it ordered five MCW Metrobuses for evaluation. No. 7001 was based at Washwood Heath along with Metrobus No. 6831. No. 7001 is seen here carrying gold West Midlands' fleetnames. The Metrobus was to win out in the end, with over 1,000 being ordered, and the five Titans were sold to London Buses, who ran a sizeable fleet of their own.

No. 7018, DOC 18V

No. 7018 is seen on the fuel pumps at Selly Oak garage while carrying WMPTE blue and cream livery. This, along with the other members of this batch of thirty Leyland National Mk 2s, would be renumbered, with No. 7018 becoming No. 1018.

No. 7048, DOC 48V

No. 7048 is seen inside Perry Barr garage under repair. There were just five of these shorter Leyland National Mk 2s in use, and most carried advertising liveries, with No. 7048 carrying Discount Warehouse livery. This small fleet, numbered 7048 to 7052, were mainly used on the 101 Centrebus route around Birmingham City Centre.

No. 8107, A107 WVP

No. 8107 is seen when brand new at Washwood Heath garage while on delivery from the nearby MCW factory. No. 8107 carries Tracline 65 livery for use on the guided busway, but it has yet to receive the guide wheels, which were placed in front of the front wheels. No. 8107 was eventually renumbered 2967 when the scheme was abandoned.

No. 8110, A110 WVP

No. 8110 is seen at the Short Heath terminus of the special Tracline 65 route. This view shows the bus on the guided busway, but the route eventually reverted back to normal bus operation. The special Metrobuses became standard buses and No. 8110 was renumbered 2970. Today No. 8110/2970 has been preserved carrying this livery.

No. M9, B63 AOP

No. M9 is seen inside Walsall garage, having just been delivered, and is seen without its Shuttlebus logos. This was a small fleet of ten Carlyle-bodied Ford Transits and they were the start of a fairly large Minibus operation in the West Midlands. No. M9 was eventually renumbered 563.

West Midlands Travel

No. 503, D503 NDA

No. 503 is seen parked inside Washwood Heath before entering service. Washwood Heath never had a Minibus allocation until Travel West Midlands days, and this Carlyle-bodied Freight Rover Sherpa bus was just passing through. The Minibus network didn't really take off until after deregulation in 1986. No. 503 is seen carrying WMPTE legal lettering, despite entering service with West Midlands Travel.

No. 531, D531 NDA

No. 531 is seen parked outside the back of Perry Barr garage on the test track. There were thirty-six of these Carlyle-bodied Freight Rover Sherpa Minibuses in use, although by this time the first thirty had been sold to Yorkshire Rider, leaving just the six with West Midlands Travel.

No. 561, B61 AOP

No. 561 is seen parked in the yard at Miller Street while carrying West Midlands Travel Mini Buzz fleetnames. Just ten of these Carlyle-bodied Ford Transits were delivered and were the first proper dedicated Minibuses to operate for the company. Some later received Chelmsley Hoppa fleetnames while based at Lea Hall. No. 561 was initially numbered M7, but was renumbered 561.

No. 572, D572 NDA

No. 572 is seen parked outside the front of Harts Hill garage, Brierley Hill. There were eighteen of these Reeve Burgess-bodied Dodge S56 Minibuses delivered to West Midlands Travel from 1986 onwards and they spent most of their lives working from Harts Hill garage, although some did end up at Walsall and with Central Liner. WMT ordered many different types of Minibuses, before ordering nearly 100 MCW Metroriders.

No. 593, D593 NDA

No. 593 is seen carrying West Midlands Travel Mini Buzz livery at Acocks Green garage. Fourteen of these Robin Hood-bodied Iveco 49.10 buses were ordered and all were based at Acocks Green for local services around Solihull. Like the Dodge S56s, some passed to Central Liner.

No. 605, D605 NOE

No. 605 is seen when brand new at the old Central Coachways yard in Lords Drive, Walsall. No. 605 was part of an order of fifty MCW-bodied Metroriders and the first members entered service at Walsall. Of note is the early attempt at route branding, something that would become more prevalent over the years.

No. 631, D631 NOE

No. 631 rests just outside the bus wash in the yard at Miller Street garage carrying the attractive silver West Midlands Travel Mini livery, which replaced the Mini Buzz blue and cream. The MCW Metrorider fleet would eventually total eighty-five buses, but unfortunately they were prone to corrosion damage and many were withdrawn and sent to the scrapyard.

No. 650, D650 NOE

No. 650 is seen at Lea Hall garage, Kitts Green having just been given a new coat of West Midlands Travel Mini livery. These Metroriders were built by local builder MCW, based in Washwood Heath, and eighty-five would eventually be ordered.

No. 1016, AOL 16T

No. 1016 is seen parked inside Birmingham Central garage. No. 1016 was initially delivered to WMPTE as No. 7016, but would be renumbered, along with rest of the single-deck fleet, into the 1xxx number series. No. 1016 carries the standard West Midlands Travel livery for the single-deck fleet, which used a lot more blue than in WMPTE days.

No. 1025, DOC 25V

No. 1025 is seen in the yard at Acocks Green having recently been repainted in the West Midlands Travel standard single-deck livery. Sister vehicle No. 1026 can be seen alongside still carrying WMPTE livery.

No. 1034, DOC 34V

No. 1034 rests in the yard outside the front of Perry Barr garage. No. 1034 was delivered as No. 7034, and it is seen carrying the newly applied single-deck livery, and is just awaiting application of the West Midlands Travel logos above the windows. No. 1034 was from a batch of thirty Leyland-bodied National 2s, and this livery really suited the styling well.

No. 1060, C60 HOM

No. 1060 is seen in Windward Way, Chelmsley Wood while operating on the 188 to Castle Vale. There were just six of these Alexander-bodied Volvo Citybuses ordered by WMPTE, and all were based in Wolverhampton. Despite this No. 1060 would find its way to Lea Hall for a period before returning to Park Lane, Wolverhampton.

No. 1063, C63 HOM

No. 1063 is seen on the fuel pumps at Lea Hall garage, Kitts Green. No. 1063 was from the initial trail batch of just six Leyland Lynxes and were ordered by WMPTE along with the six Volvo Citybuses for evaluating. The Lynx won out in the end, with an order for 250 buses. Note the Gardner turbo badge fitted to the front of No. 1063, and also the WMPTE and West Midlands Travel logos on the side.

No. 1064, C64 HOM

No. 1064 is seen on private hire duty at the Model Railway Museum, Pendon, Oxfordshire. No. 1064 is seen carrying the silver West Midlands Travel livery, which was carried by all the production Leyland Lynxes. This initial batch of six Lynxes had different engines and gearboxes from the production batch.

West Midlands PTE and Its Successors

No. 1476, ROK 476M

No. 1476 is seen parked outside the front of West Bromwich garage. No. 1476 was from a batch of sixty Leyland Nationals and was originally delivered as No. 4476 before being renumbered. West Bromwich always had a large allocation of single-deck vehicles, and the Nationals would be replaced by Volvo B6LEs and Mercedes-Benz O405Ns.

No. 1491, TOE 491N

No. 1491 is seen carrying the standard West Midlands Travel single-deck livery while parked inside Yardley Wood garage. WMPTE was a big user of the Leyland National, ordering both versions, the Mk 1 and Mk 2.

No. 1806, OOX 806R

No. 1806 is seen inside Selly Oak garage, having recently been repainted in the standard single-deck livery. Selly Oak garage would close as an operational garage in 1986 but would see further use as a storage facility for withdrawn buses awaiting resale or scrapping.

No. 1822, OOX 822R

No. 1822 is seen inside Washwood Heath garage having just been released from works overhaul at Tyburn Road. No. 1822 was one of the dual-purpose seated Leyland Nationals and as such was repainted into West Midlands Travel Timesaver livery, in which it can be seen. No. 1822 is just waiting the application of transfers and was allocated to Lea Hall garage at the time, Washwood Heath not having a single-deck allocation until the Leyland Lynxes arrived for the 94 route.

West Midlands PTE and Its Successors

No. 2021, BOK 21V

No. 2021 is seen at rest in the yard at Birmingham Central garage. This garage used to be known as Liverpool Street in WMPTE days and was renamed Birmingham Central. No. 2021 was initially allocated to Sandy Lane garage, Coventry, but moved to Birmingham early in its career.

No. 2034, BOK 34V

No. 2034 is seen parked inside Washwood Heath garage, having just been released from works overhaul. The overhaul included a repaint into the new West Midlands Travel silver livery, which was quite a startling change from the blue and cream livery that had been on the streets of Birmingham for so many years. This was Washwood Heath's first bus to carry this livery.

No. 2035, BOK 35V

No. 2035 is seen inside Washwood Heath on the same day as the previous photograph and this too had not long been to works for overhaul, but this would become Washwood Heath's last bus to receive blue and cream livery, with the first silver bus, No. 2034, seen parked in front.

No. 2168, GOG 168W

No. 2168 is seen parked inside the then relatively new Wheatley Street garage, Coventry. This was one of Coventry's first repaints into silver livery, with the majority of buses still retaining the blue and cream at this time. No. 2168 spent many years based in Coventry, before moving to Birmingham.

No. 2175, GOG 175W

No. 2175 is seen parked outside the front of Perry Barr garage. No. 2175 carries blue and cream livery with West Midlands Travel logos, and unusually has had the front number plate repositioned to where a Mk 2 Metrobus's number plate would be. This bus started life at Washwood Heath garage, just a stone's throw from where it was built.

No. 2189, GOG 189W

No. 2189 is seen inside Washwood Heath garage having just had the West Midlands Travel logos applied, replacing the WMPTE logos, although it still retains WMPTE legal lettering.

No. 2190, GOG 190W

No. 2190 is seen being pulled out of the paint booth at Tyburn Road Works, Erdington. No. 2190 has already had the silver applied, including the red stripe around the top, and has just had the blue applied. No. 2190 was allocated to Washwood Heath at the time and Tyburn Road works has now been closed and demolished.

No. 2210, GOG 210W

No. 2210 is seen drying off after paying a visit to the paint booth at Tyburn Road works, Erdington. With such a large fleet, the turnaround time in the paint shop was always short. No. 2210 was allocated to West Bromwich garage at the time.

West Midlands PTE and Its Successors

No. 2231, GOG 231W

No. 2231 is seen waiting its turn in the paint booth at Tyburn Road works, Erdington. No. 2231 has already had its widows covered over and would soon enter the paint shop to receive a repaint into silver. No. 2231 was allocated to Acocks Green garage at the time and was one of a batch of twenty Mk 1 Metrobuses to have Rolls-Royce engines, following evaluation of two prototypes.

No. 2438, NOA 438X

No. 2438 is seen parked inside West Bromwich garage, advertising the now defunct Birmingham Super Prix. No. 2438 was just the third Mk 2 Metrobus delivered to WMPTE, but by this time had changed to West Midlands Travel.

No. 2590, POG 590Y

No. 2590 is seen inside Washwood Heath garage on the day it received its new West Midlands Travel logos, replacing the WMPTE logos. No. 2590 was part of a batch of fifteen Metrobuses delivered to Washwood Heath, which helped with the withdrawal of some early Fleetlines.

No. 2877, B877 DOM

No. 2877 is seen parked up in Pool Meadow bus station, Coventry. This was another early repaint into silver livery for a Coventry-based MCW Metrobus. This used to be a favourite spot to see the buses parked up in Coventry, but now the bus station has been completely rebuilt.

No. 2925, D925 NDA

No. 2925 is seen parked in the yard at Lea Hall garage, Kitts Green, in front of two sister MCW Metrobuses. No. 2925 carries the very attractive French blue Timesaver livery, which certainly made these dual-purpose seated buses stand out.

No. 2926, D926 NDA

No. 2926 is seen parked in exactly the same place as No. 2925 in the previous photo, but this was taken some time before as the French Blue livery carried by No. 2925 replaced this version of the Timesaver livery.

No. 2937, D937 NDA

No. 2937 is seen inside West Bromwich garage having been jacked up to have its tyres removed. No. 2937 still carries the original Timesaver livery, which, when revealed in 1986, was a dramatic change from the traditional blue and cream livery worn for so many years.

No. 2956, D956 NDA

No. 2956 is seen on the left of three dual-purpose MCW Metrobuses in the yard at Birmingham Central garage. All three carry different Timesaver liveries, with No. 2932 in the centre being the original, followed by No. 2958 on the right carrying the red stripe version, and No. 2956 was an experimental version, but this would be replaced by the French Blue livery.

No. 3049, F49 XOF

No. 3049 is seen on rally duty at Blackpool. At the time, No. 3049 was chosen to receive ESOP livery at Washwood Heath and as such was used on a lot of rallies for a number of years, replacing WHs No. 6666 on these duties. Each garage received an ESOP-liveried Metrobus, celebrating the employee buyout of the company. Washwood Heath only ever had two Mk 2a Metrobuses – this and No. 3050.

No. 3060, F60 XOF

No. 3060 is seen inside West Bromwich garage, alongside fellow Mk 2a Metrobus No. 3066. Both are seen still looking very clean and both are up on jacks for attention.

No. 4041, XON 41J

No. 4041 is seen outside Washwood Heath garage carrying West Midlands Travel logos. This is the only time that this bus has carried these logos, having had them specially applied while at Washwood Heath, during which time it was being prepared for handing over to the Aston Manor Transport Museum. The logos were quickly changed back to WMPTE ones by the museum.

No. 4583, GOG 583N

No. 4583 is seen parked outside the rear of Perry Barr garage on the test track. By this time, this Park Royal-bodied Daimler Fleetline had been relegated to training bus duty.

West Midlands PTE and Its Successors

No. 4624, JOV 624P

No. 4624 rests in the yard at Acocks Green garage. No. 4624 shows signs of having been to Sandy Lane works, Coventry, for a mid-life overhaul – the sign being the small blue stripe above the front windscreens. The area upon which No. 4624 stands is now where the maintenance facility is at Acocks Green.

No. 4749, JOV 749P

No. 4749 is seen parked outside the front of Perry Barr garage. This was one of fifty Alexander-bodied Ailsa Volvo B55-10 buses ordered by WMPTE following trials with three Ailsas. No. 4749 carries the lighter shade of blue that was applied to some of this fleet following deregulation. All fifty would be sold to London Buses.

No. 4785, JOV 785P

No. 4785 stands outside Perry Barr garage having been repainted into the Metrobus style of livery. This livery was only applied after changing to West Midlands Travel and all fifty of the production Alexander-bodied Ailsa Volvo B55-10s would be sold to London Buses.

No. 6306, KON 306P

No. 6306 is seen at the Solihull station terminus of the number 6 route. No. 6306 carries the lighter shade of blue, applied after deregulation. No. 6306 was later sold on for further use, and ended up in Ireland.

No. 6391, NOC 391R

No. 6391 is seen parked on the test track outside the rear of Perry Barr garage. This facility was fantastic, being set up exactly how it would be out on the road for trainee drivers. The track was used to park vehicles when not in use. No. 6391 carries the lighter shade of blue and was waiting its new West Midlands Travel logos.

No. 6429, NOC 429R

No. 6429 is seen at rest in the yard at Dudley garage. This garage was to close and be demolished to make way for a dual carriageway. No. 6429 is still around today, having been converted to a partial open-top bus, and is an MCW-bodied Leyland Fleetline.

No. 6494, NOC 494R

No. 6494 is seen in a withdrawn state outside the front of Hockley garage. At this time an inroad was being made into withdrawing the Fleetlines, with No. 6494 being an MCW-bodied Leyland example.

No. 6630, SDA 630S

No. 6630 is seen being driven through the streets of Wolverhampton by an engineer, possibly on the way to a break-down, or just out on test from Cleveland Road garage. No. 6630 was a Park Royal-bodied Leyland Fleetline, with the body styles between both Park Royal and MCW being very similar.

No. 6666, WDA 666T

No. 6666 is seen parked outside the front of Washwood Heath garage. This Park Royal-bodied Leyland Fleetline was from the last batch of Fleetlines delivered to WMPTE and was adopted by Washwood Heath as its rally bus. It is seen having just been repainted into the red stripe livery, but was painted grey not silver.

No. 6732, NOC 732R

No. 6732 rests inside Wheatley Street garage, Coventry. No. 6732 still retains the WMPTE blue, rather than the lighter shade that West Midlands Travel adopted. This is an East Lancs-bodied Leyland Fleetline and is one of forty in the batch.

No. 6833, SDA 833S

No. 6833 is seen parked in the yard at Dudley garage. This was the third of seven prototype MCW Metrobuses delivered to WMPTE in 1978. Six were fitted out like Fleetlines inside, with red seats and blue Formica, while No. 6835 was fitted with the more familiar orange and brown seating. These prototypes eventually lead to orders for over 1,100 Metrobuses being placed.

No. 6917, WDA 917T

No. 6917 is seen parked inside Perry Barr garage. Of note is the former Sandy Lane 'S' above the drivers windscreen and also the fleet number on the side is still in its original position, having yet to be moved above the driver's window.

No. 6951, WDA 951T

No. 6951 is seen inside Washwood Heath garage on the day it received its new West Midlands Travel logos, which had replaced the WMPTE logos. Today most of Washwood Heath has been demolished and has been replaced with a supermarket. Washwood Heath was the first garage that I was based at as a driver.

No. 7000, WDA 700T

No. 7000 is seen inside Washwood Heath garage having just been released from Tyburn Road works. This MCW-bodied Leyland Fleetline was just stopping off on its way to Perry Barr garage, having just been transferred from Dudley, and is seen running on trade plates, with the front number plate missing.

No. 8101, A101 WVP

No. 8101 is seen outside Birmingham Airport while on promotional duty. This former Tracline 65 MCW Metrobus was chosen to showcase the new Time Saver livery, which would start after deregulation. This was later renumbered 2961.

No. 8102, A102 WVP

No. 8102 is seen in Upper Bull Street, Birmingham, carrying its special Tracline 65 livery. This route was chosen as a guided busway, but by this time the experiment had finished and the busway was grassed over. The vehicles lost their guided wheels and soon became ordinary MCW Metrobuses, with No. 8102 being renumbered 2962.

No. 8753, SDA 753S

No. 8753 is seen parked on the test track outside the back of Perry Barr garage. This East Lancs-bodied Leyland Fleetline was in use as a driver trainer at the time, hence the renumbering from 6753.

WM Buses

No. 665, E665 RVP

No. 665 is seen parked outside the front of West Bromwich garage. This MCW-bodied Metrorider carries the livery of Smiths Your Bus and when it carried this livery it was based in Burton-upon-Trent. When the Burton operation finished, No. 665 was transferred back to West Bromwich but still retained the Your Bus livery and had WM Buses West Bromwich fleetnames applied.

No. 806, K916 FVC

No. 806 rests in the yard at Park Lane garage, Wolverhampton. This Plaxton-bodied Dennis Dart started life with Your Bus, in Alcester, before being taken over by West Midlands Travel. It was put into use at Park Lane along with a couple of sister vehicles during the WM Buses period. It was eventually sold and was used by Stagecoach but was scrapped following collision damage.

No. 1015, AOL 15T

No. 1015 is seen parked in the yard at Park Lane garage, Wolverhampton. No. 1015 was delivered to WMPTE as No. 7015 and carried plain cream livery. It was part of a batch of ten Leyland Nationals. By the time of the photo it was based at Park Lane, who had quite a sizeable allocation of Nationals, but they were to be replaced by Optare Excels and Volvo B10Bs. Alongside is Alexander-bodied Volvo Citybus No. 1060.

No. 1287, G287 EOG

No. 1287 is seen parked in between the main garage at Hockley and the administration building. At this time the fleet was branded as WM Buses and each bus was given its own garage allocation in the fleetname. This only lasted a few years, before the Travel West Midlands names began to appear. This Leyland Lynx was one of 250 ordered by West Midlands Travel and all have now left the fleet, with a lot sold to Highland Country and Bus Eireann in Ireland, where No. 1287 ended its days.

No. 1322, M322 LJW

No. 1322 is seen parked in the yard at Park Lane garage, Wolverhampton. There were just six of these Alexander-bodied Volvo B10Bs in use and all were allocated to Park Lane. This view shows the WM Buses fleetname, which would have to be replaced when a bus was transferred between garages, although these six Volvos spent their entire lives at Wolverhampton.

No. 1518, GOK 618N

No. 1518 spends a quiet Sunday parked in the yard at Park Lane garage, Wolverhampton. This Leyland National was unusual in that it was delivered with an out of sequence registration compared to the rest of the batch of sixty Nationals. When originally delivered, No. 1518 carried the number 4518.

No. 2098, GOG 98W

No. 2098 is seen up on the jacks at Lea Hall garage, Kitts Green, having been unceremoniously de-roofed after going under a low bridge. There have been a few buses in the West Midlands that have suffered this fate, although by strange coincidence sister vehicle No. 2097 was also de-roofed, but was repaired. No. 2098 would be withdrawn and scrapped following this incident, and was photographed being stripped for spares.

No. 2130, GOG 130W
No. 2130 is seen parked in the yard at Perry Barr garage. No. 2130 had just been released from works overhaul, including a repaint into the silver version of the red stripe livery. When clean this livery suited the styling of the Mk 1 Metrobuses well. Of note is the fact that No. 2130 has had its front fog lamps removed, whereas sister vehicle No. 2337 behind still carries them.

No. 2508, POG 508Y
No. 2508 is seen parked outside Perry Barr garage, having not long been repainted. No. 2508 carries WM Buses fleetnames, and again this livery suited the Mk 2 Metrobuses just as well as on the Mk 1s. No. 2508 is parked on what used to be the test track out the back of Perry Barr garage. No. 2508 ended its days being used by De Courcey in Coventry.

No. 3030, F30 XOF

No. 3030 is seen at Perry Barr on a dull and dismal Sunday. This Mk 2a MCW Metrobus was chosen by Perry Barr to receive the heritage Birmingham City transport livery, with each garage having a bus repainted into heritage colours, including Walsall, Wolverhampton, West Bromwich and Coventry.

No. 6735, NOC 735R

No. 6735 is seen on the fuel pumps at Walsall garage. This was from a batch of forty Leyland Fleetlines delivered with East Lancs bodywork, initially at Acocks Green and also at the two Coventry garages. Eventually all were allocated to Wheatley Street garage, Coventry, but later on in life eleven were transferred to Walsall garage to end their careers.

No. 6957, WDA 957T

No. 6957 is seen in the yard at Lea Hall garage, Kitts Green. This MCW-bodied Leyland Fleetline carries WM Buses Washwood Heath fleetnames, as at the time it was allocated to Washwood Heath, but was on loan to Lea Hall for the day. With these two garages being close together, it was easy to loan buses between garages. No. 6957 carries the mainly grey West Midlands Travel livery, which basically just replaced the WMPTE era cream with grey. At this time Lea Hall had lost its allocation of Fleetlines.

No. 6988, WDA 988T

No. 6988 is seen parked alongside the garage at Wheatley Street, Coventry. Wheatley Street was built to replace the two old garages in Coventry – Sandy Lane and Harnall Lane – bringing both allocations under the one roof. Coventry has always had a large Fleetline presence and this MCW-bodied Leyland example is seen carrying WM Buses fleetnames.

Park Lane View

A general view of the parking area outside the back of Park Lane garage, Wolverhampton. In view are twenty MCW-bodied Metrobuses, both of the Mk 1 and Mk 2 variety, and also five Wright-bodied Volvo B10Bs. This view shows how many buses could be parked here, with most rows two or three deep. The B10Bs, and sister types B10Ls, along with their smaller counterparts, the B6Ls, were the start of the long run-down of many traditional buses in the West Midlands, but most have now also been replaced and scrapped.

Travel West Midlands

No. 669, F669 YOG

MCW Metrorider No. 669 is seen parked outside the back of West Bromwich garage. By this time the company had changed its name to Travel West Midlands, which resulted in another fleet-wide rebranding exercise. No. 669 shares space with other Metroriders, No. 666 and No. 613, which carries all-over adverts for Riva Bingo.

West Midlands PTE and Its Successors

No. 683, F683 YOG

No. 683 is seen parked up the side of Washwood Heath garage, carrying Travel West Midlands livery. Washwood Heath had a very small allocation of MCW Metroriders for use on the No. 693 service around Castle Bromwich and they would eventually be replaced by new Alexander-bodied Mercedes 0814Ds.

No. 1039, DOC 39V

No. 1039 is seen parked in the huge yard at Park Lane garage, Wolverhampton. This was one of a handful of Mk 2 Leyland Nationals that were converted to dual-door specification for use around the newly opened ICC in Birmingham. They later passed to Park Lane for use of the 500 Town Centre Free Bus. No. 1039 carries a mixture of fleet names; WM Buses on the front, and Travel West Midlands on the side. No. 1039 was delivered as No. 7039 before being renumbered 1039.

No. 1055, C55 HOM

No. 1055 is seen up on the jacks inside Park Lane garage, Wolverhampton. There were six of these Alexander-bodied Volvo Citybuses introduced by West Midlands Travel alongside six Leyland Lynxes for evaluation purposes, with the Lynxes being the preferred option.

No. 1144, G144 EOG

No. 1144 is seen parked at Walsall garage ready for another turn of duty the following day. No. 1144 was part of an order of 250 Leyland Lynxes that was placed following the initial trial of six earlier buses. By this time the Lynxes were starting to look a little rough around the edges.

West Midlands PTE and Its Successors

No. 1247, G247 EOG

No. 1247 is seen at rest inside Lea Hall garage, Kitts Green. Lea Hall had a sizeable allocation of these buses for use on various routes that had low bridges, including the long 71 route. The Lynxes were quick off the mark to drive, but were let down by their infuriating rattles.

No. 1317, M317 LJW

No. 1317 rests in the yard at Park Lane garage, Wolverhampton. This Alexander-bodied Volvo B10B was part of a small order of just six buses and all were based at Park Lane for their whole lives, with all eventually being scrapped, although one, No. 1321, was withdrawn with severe fire damage.

No. 1850, TVP 850S

No. 1850 is seen parked inside Park Lane garage, Wolverhampton. This Leyland National was from a batch of thirty Nationals delivered, with half being bus-seated, and the other fifteen delivered with dual-purpose seating. No. 1850 was the last of the bus-seated examples, and was delivered as No. 6850 before being renumbered 1850.

No. 2016, BOK 16V

No. 2016 is seen up in the air on the lifting jacks at Park Lane garage, Wolverhampton. No. 2016 was initially delivered to Harnall Lane garage, Coventry, spending most of its life in the Coventry area before making the long trek across to Wolverhampton.

No. 2032, BOK 32V

No. 2032 is seen inside Lea Hall garage, Kitts Green. This Mk 1 MCW Metrobus was delivered to Washwood Heath and would eventually pass to the Your Bus fleet at Miller Street. It later transferred back to the main fleet, being based at Lea Hall. This bus was different in having black window surrounds on both decks and also at this time stood out by having a working set of front fog lamps.

No. 2159, GOG 159W

No. 2159 basks in the sunshine at the Central Coachways yard at Miller Street. This Mk 1 Metrobus had been on loan to the Bee Line Company in Manchester and upon its return entered the Central Coachways fleet, in whose livery it carries. It would later gain Travel Your Bus fleetnames.

No. 2166, GOG 166W

No. 2166 is seen in the yard at Hockley garage. This Mk 1 Metrobus spent many years based at Coventry before moving west in the 1990s and was one of just a couple of Metrobuses to receive Fleetline-style destination panels, presumably following collision damage – the other one being No. 2325. No. 2166 would be sold to McColls of Balloch, a large user of withdrawn West Midlands Metrobuses.

No. 2252, GOG 252W

No. 2252 is seen inside Hockley garage carrying route branding for the 101 route. At this time Mk 1 Metrobuses were not common carriers of route branding – TWM preferring to use the Mk 2 version instead – with just No. 2248 and No. 2335 at Washwood Heath being branded for 590 use as well. I was never a big fan of the route branding idea, especially in this form.

No. 2475, NOA 475X

No. 2475 is seen in the yard at Birmingham Central garage carrying Travel West Midlands logos. This Mk 2 Metrobus spent most of its life based at Quinton garage, moving to Birmingham Central when Quinton closed. Alongside can be seen the new influx of Volvo B10L buses carrying the new white low-floor livery.

No. 2496, POG 496Y

No. 2496 is seen parked in the sunshine in the yard at Park Lane garage, Wolverhampton. This Mk 2 MCW-bodied Metrobus had not long been returned to service following a repaint into the grey version of Travel West Midlands livery, with a silver-liveried sister alongside. At this time the wing mirrors were painted red, which improved their appearance. No. 2496 was eventually saved for preservation and has been superbly restored to West Midlands Travel blue and cream livery.

No. 2540, POG 540Y

No. 2540 is seen alongside the bus wash in the yard at Birmingham Central garage. No. 2540 has just been released from works overhaul, including a repaint into the grey version of the TWM livery, and also of note is the lack of destination blinds, as it had recently been transferred in from the closed Quinton garage. No. 2540 later saw use in Leicester following its withdrawal from service.

No. 2638, ROX 638Y

No. 2638 is seen outside the works at Walsall garage. This Mk 2 Metrobus had just returned from Marshalls in Cambridge, who had won a contract to rebuild the back ends of the Metrobuses following corrosion damage. Most, if not all, of the Mk 2s visited Cambridge for this work to be done and were repainted upon their return to the West Midlands. No. 2638 spent its entire life working out of Wolverhampton.

No. 2932, D932 NDA

No. 2932 stands in the Central Coachways yard at Miller Street garage. This Mk 2 Metrobus was one of fifty delivered with coach seating to West Midlands Travel in 1986 following deregulation. It is seen having been transferred to the Central Liner fleet, as it still carried the coach seats. Alongside can be seen fellow coach-seated examples No. 2921 and No. 2938. This batch of Metrobuses was easily recognisable in only having a single-height destination screen, rather than the usual two.

No. 2948, D948 NDA

No. 2948 is seen parked outside the front of Perry Barr garage. This Mk 2 Metrobus was one of the coach-seated examples. This batch were delivered for the Timesaver network of routes and were some of the best Metrobuses I had ever driven, as not only did they have coach seats, they also had an extra gear, meaning they were a lot quicker than the ordinary Metrobuses in the fleet. No. 2948 later entered the driver training fleet working for Travel London.

No. 3014, F314 XOF

No. 3014 stands outside the old works at Walsall garage. No. 3014 was from the last batch of 150 MCW-bodied Metrobuses delivered to West Midlands Travel. They were slightly improved and were known as Mk 2as. The final part of this batch was held up in their delivery from MCW following legal wrangling. This batch also had larger number blinds in their destination screens, compared to the other Mk 2 Metrobuses.

No. 3058, F58 XOF

No. 3058 is seen going for a spin through the bus wash in the yard of Park Lane garage, Wolverhampton. This Mk 2a Metrobus spent its entire career working in Wolverhampton and survived quite late, not being withdrawn until 2009. Park Lane garage housed a large allocation of Metrobuses at this time, but most were eventually replaced by Tridents.

No. 3218, H218 LOM

No. 3218 is seen parked in the yard at Birmingham Central garage carrying Travel West Midlands livery. Alongside is Birmingham City Transport Heritage-liveried sister, No. 3225. These buses were from a batch of forty Alexander-bodied Scania N113s and all were based at Birmingham Central for their entire lives. At this time each garage had a Metrobus painted into heritage liveries, although Central had No. 3225 done as the TWM-owned Daimler CVG6 No. 3225, as the running number is the same.